THE KEY TO GENERATIONAL WEALTH

A GUIDE ON HOW TO BUILD LASTING WEALTH FOR YOU AND YOUR FAMILY.

WRITTEN BY

D. CHRISTOPHER

THE KEY TO
GENERATIONAL WEALTH

D. CHRISTOPHER

CONTENTS

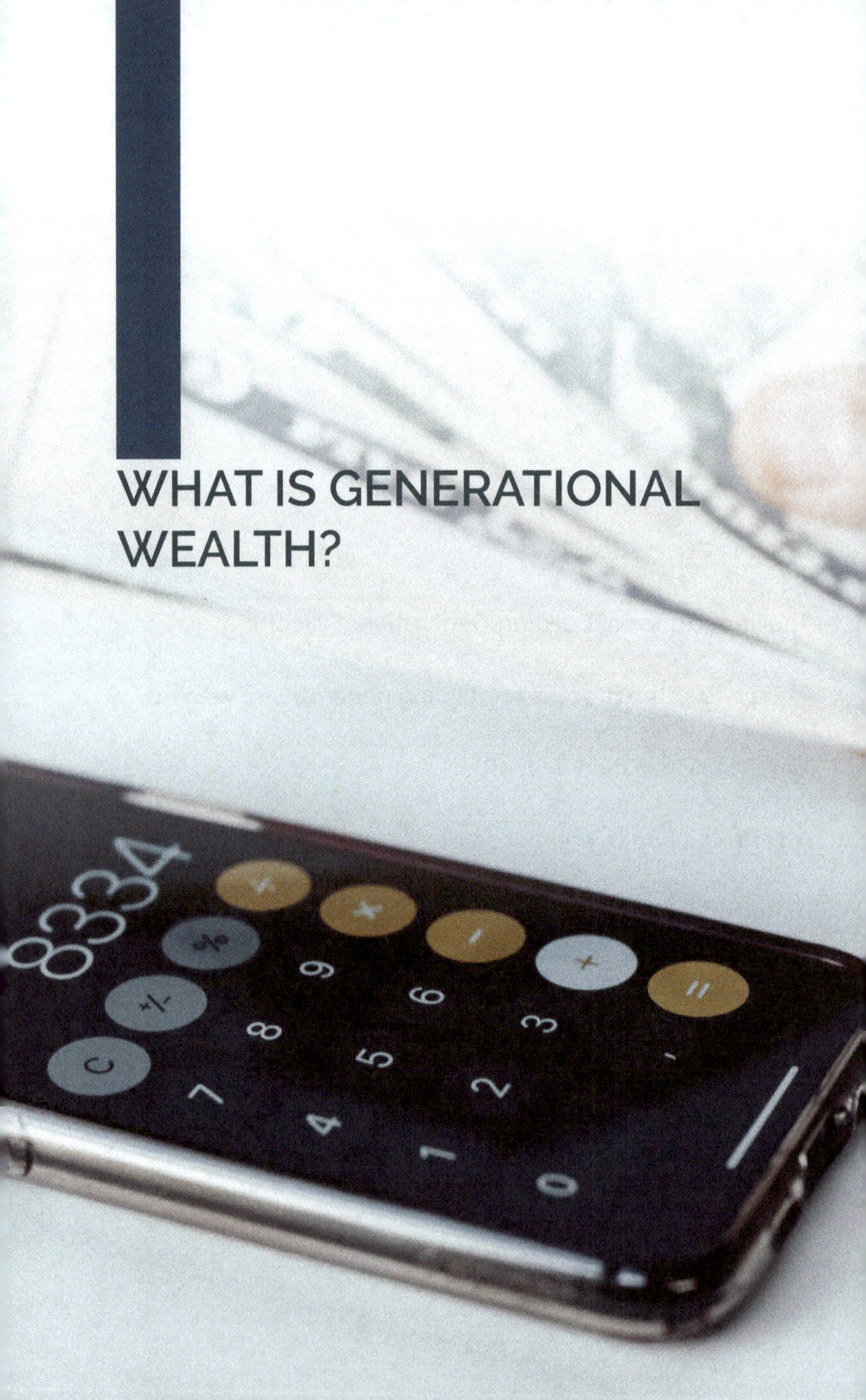
WHAT IS GENERATIONAL WEALTH?

Generational wealth, also known as family legacy or family wealth, is wealth that gets transferred from one generation of a family to the next. It can occur on the death of a parent or other family member, or during the life of both people. It is essentially wealth that is passed down from one generation to the next. If you are able to leave something behind for your children or grandchildren, then you are contributing to the growth of generational wealth in your family.

Of course, we all leave things such as memories and healthy genetics. However, generational wealth has to do with the financial resources that you are able to leave behind.

Generational wealth starts when general wealth is passed down within a family, from one generation to the next. The first generation accumulates assets (money or property) during their lifetime, which they then pass down to their children. With proper planning, those children can then pass down that wealth and additionally obtained assets to their own children, so on and so forth.

Lastly, Generational wealth is the key to freedom. The more wealth passed down from generation to generation, the more freedom of choice is passed down. Freedom from working an everyday 9-5 job out of necessity. Freedom to pursue ones ultimate passions. Freedom to travel and experience the wonders of the world without having any obligations on your time, energy and most importantly strain on your finances.

I know, I know..you're thinking "Well why do I have to do all of the hard work?" Well, simply put the more work you do to create generational wealth today the easier your life will begin to become tomorrow. Going through each step, will absolutely better your current financial position.

Wealth accumulation is of interest for several reasons. At the household level, wealth provides a source of future consumption, as well as insurance against adverse economic occurrences. At the aggregate level, wealth finances current investments, affects current consumption spending, and improves the chances of overall success of financial decisions.

Generational wealth can be in the form of cash savings, property, life insurance, investments and even now crypto-currency. It can even be in the form of a family-owned business or valuable possessions such as artwork, antiques and jewelry.

Today we are going to focus on only four types of generational wealth: Investing, Real Estate, Launching a Business and Safely Investing in Crypto-currency.

While the points noted are effective when applied and have been effective for me personally. I am in no way claiming to be a financial advisor. I am simply, sharing my real-life experiences and knowledge with you so that you can gain a better understanding of wealth creation. Everyone's individual financial situation is unique to them. I always recommend speaking to a Certified Financial Planner or other qualified financial professional to ensure that anything you decide to do that may be referenced here, will be of benefit for you.

THE IMPORTANCE OF BUILDING GENERATIONAL WEALTH

If you are just starting to positively shape your finances, or starting out with a large debt burden, then that is the first key to achieving generational wealth. Wealth again, is obtained through passing down assets, not debt. So Congratulations! Keep going and always remember to carry as little debt as possible. There are methods for using debt to obtain things that are considered assets, but we'll talk more on that later!

If your parents could have been able to fund your college education, instead of you playing catch up to pay down your student loan debt, you could be saving for your first home or investing towards your future early retirement. This would have made your financial future more stable and put you way ahead of the game by about 30 years. Its ok though, no worries, the number one factor to achieving success in wealth creation, START! Going forward, no more "If's" and/or "but's"... lets get to it.

By preparing for your child's future today, you're able to help them get a running start on their own financial future. That's what it means to build generational wealth. It is creating a solid foundation for the future financial success of your descendants, which they can then continue to build upon for further generations.

The benefits of generational wealth bring financial security to the family. The generation that is taking over doesn't need to take on too much debt. When wealth is present, they are also empowered with the means to increase their earnings free of debt. In turn, future generations can use their assets to grow their wealth and leave money and property to their family.

Generational wealth also benefits the communities in which we live in some cases. At some point our remaining family may decide to invest in a new business or grow an existing business. Small family run businesses are the cornerstones of many communities. They employ other people to run the business, giving those employees and their families greater financial security. When they spend their money (hopefully they also save some!), they boost the country's economic growth. After all, small businesses are the backbone of the countries economy.

An inheritance can offer substantial resources when one is also just starting out. It can teach your children or grandchildren how to be independent and resourceful. A financial boost at the right time can also help remove some of the pressure that prevents innovation and distracts them from going after their dreams. While you have worked hard your entire life to grow your wealth, it is entirely feasible that your descendants will experience greater hardships and less success, and may struggle to make ends meet. Not for lack of trying but simply because prices and service costs will be inflated higher then than they are now. Generational wealth, accumulated and handed down by ones ancestors, is a privilege that a lucky few are able to enjoy.

Through setting up Inheritance Trust Funds, instead of providing an financial inheritance outright, parents and grandparents can use the funds to create an incentive by establishing trust conditions through their financial advisors or estate planning specialists. This strategy allows them to choose the conditions under which their assets are passed onto the next generation. For example, heirs may be required to complete a degree program to receive a lump sum or use the trust only for specified purposes, such as to start a business or purchase a home also in the name of the family trust. This allows you to shape how the assets you leave behind actively benefit those who receive them.

Generational wealth isn't a one-off inheritance that you spend in your lifetime, neither is it only for the super wealthy. Generational wealth is about making your money work for you and your family across generations, and you can start the process, whoever you are.

People with Generational Wealth have access to the best doctors, which can mean better health and a longer life — and more years to grow that wealth. They often own homes in better neighborhoods where the values appreciate significantly over time, leading to greater wealth attainment. Also, the generationally wealthy can afford top-notch education. Add it all up, and you'll notice that people with generational wealth don't have as many obstacles impeding upon their success.

Resource centers on financial literacy

Nearly a generation ago, organizations like the Ford Foundation and The Generational Wealth Foundation pivoted to focus much of their economic programming on expanding opportunities to build wealth, through promising but untested approaches to asset building.

Scholarly research, such as Michael Sherraden's, Assets and the Poor (1991) and Melvin Oliver and Thomas Shapiro's, Black Wealth/White Wealth (1995), have shared the powerful consequences of lacking wealth, as opposed to merely lacking income. Their research has also called out the stark racial wealth gap that persists in America.

The Generational Wealth Foundation is a non-profit organization, headquartered in Atlanta, GA, which uniquely offers a holistic approach to supporting wealth generation, through financial literacy programming, coupled with lifestyle skill development among youth and adults. Their mission is to foster wealth principles among socio- economically diverse populations, and reduce the wealth gap.

A STEP-BY-STEP PROCESS TO BUILDING GENERATIONAL WEALTH

Through building generational wealth, you can make sure your children and grandchildren have financial stability without financial stress.

Building generational wealth takes careful planning, commitment, time and discipline – but it is possible and well worth the effort.

Teaching your children to be good stewards of their money is key to passing wealth down through generations. To put it simply: Ignorance is not bliss when it comes to money management and creating wealth.

You don't have to be rich or any economics major, but one should aspire to know the basics of budgeting, savings, retirement planning, and investing. You should also understand the difference between assets and liabilities, and the importance of a budget worksheet and a good credit score.

Step 1 - Financial Literacy Financial literacy is the number one key to creating your own wealth.

It is important to understand how to budget, how to save, how compound interest works and why having your money just sitting in the bank at a low interest rate is diminishing your wealth potential over time.

If you are the first in your family to start generating wealth, it is important to educate yourself and your family. If you are not sharing your financial knowledge and experience with your children, then you are creating obstacles against wealth creation in our family.

Lest start with your bank or credit union. Most banks and credit unions have financial-planning services that are free for customers or members. Additionally, The Federal Deposit Insurance Commission (FDIC) offers free resources for financial literacy and money management through its Money Smart program that teaches you how to save and invest.

What is an asset?

An asset is a resource, either real, financial or non-monetarily identifiable, that contains value to an individual or company for future use or benefit.

Some Examples include:

- Cash and equivalents
- Real Estate/Land
- Cars and Trucks
- Art and Jewelry
- Patents and Intellectual Property

What is a liability?

A liability is a debt obligation owed by an individual or company to another party from which it was borrowed. This debt is often satisfied as a payment over time either monthly, quarterly or yearly.

Some Examples include:

- Credit Card Obligations
- Bank Loans (Car Loans, Home Loans, Personal/Payday Loans)
- Unpaid Bills/Collection Accounts

What is compound interest?

When you earn interest yields(additional earnings) on the money you have saved and interest you've earned.

Example:

You save $2,000 (principal) and it earns 3% interest

once a year (compounding frequency) = **$2,060 after 1 year.**

($2,000 x 3% = $60 / $2,000+60 = $2,060).

Year 2 = ($2,060 x 3% = 61.80/$2,060+61.80 = **$2,121.80**)

As you can see, compounding interest is an amazing tool to essentially create additional wealth from your savings, by simply using the power of time. The key here, is to make sure that you choose a Savings account (or High-Yield Checking) account that offers you the highest interest rate yields. There are several institutions (check your current institution first) that offer these types of accounts such as Ally Bank, Citibank, Synchrony Bank, Goldman Sachs etc. The caveat here is to AVOID regular withdrawals, you are placing your money in these accounts to gain interest over time, so the longer you let your money sit the more it will grow. Additionally, **be sure to read the fine print when signing up,** because these accounts offer higher interest rate yields, they tend to have penalties associated with overly frequent withdrawals and/or monthly fees if your account balance does not meet a monthly minimum.

How do I save?

This is one of the toughest questions to answer, so I will simply start by saying this. Saving starts with really taking the time to dive deep into our own personal habits. Aside from generating income, which is important, our saving habits must start with understanding how we spend our money. Taking a look back

1-month really gives you a current picture of where your money is going. If you can go back 3-months that's even better because then you can start to notice trends in your spending habits. I will admit, when I received this advice I was reluctant because it seemed so tedious and boring. However, I had no choice and decided to bite. When I tell you I was so ashamed of myself, shocked and enlightened at the same time by what I saw and what I learned. In one month alone I had spent over $1200 on DoorDash. Can you believe that! That was entire extra rent payment on having food delivered. It was all down-hill from there because I knew I could absolutely cut that out every month and save it instead.

From there, I just kept going, $115 every month on subscriptions (Hulu, Netflix, Tinder, Apple Music, Tidal) the list goes on and on. Once you have a better picture of where your money is going every month, you can easily develop a plan to change those habits of spending and flip them towards habits of saving.

The next step here is to automate your savings. This can be achieved by having multiple bank accounts open that each serve their own purpose. A few that I have are marked for

Emergencies, Travel and Entertainment/Dining Out. I have direct deposit at work so each pay period I have a set amount going into each account automatically for me. If I want to buy a plane ticket, I only use funds within my Travel Account. If its empty, I don't go on the trip, send the text to my friends "Sorry, I cant make this one." and then move on. If I want to "DoorDash" but the $100 every month I deposit has been depleted, I get my butt up and go cook or make a sandwich. I make it easy on myself and hold myself accountable because at the end of it all, I have a goal. That goal may upset my friends, who are still going to have a great time without me, but if I go against MY goal I know I will over extend myself and I will have to pay the price later, not them.

If you don't have access to a bank you can do so using the envelope trick. Go and buy a box of 100 envelopes. Take a few envelopes and mark each envelope with a goal (Emergency Savings, Travel, Down Payment, etc.). In each envelope place $20 each week, place it in a box or somewhere safe that you can't access. On the last week of the year, you will place a final deposit of $20 and will have grown your savings to $1,040. You can use those funds at the end of the year towards whatever goals you have set for them, whether that be a trip or a down payment on a car or home or just to build an emergency fund. The goal here is just to simplify your saving.

What is a budget?

A budget is a plan that enables you to create financial freedom. A budget allows you to pre-plan and track your expenses against your monthly incoming coming in. This will help you generate a visual map so that you can pay bills on time, know how much every month you need to put towards building your emergency fund, how much you need to save for large purchases such as a car or house and how much you are spending on debt payments. In summary, a budget will help you understand your financial position every month and empower you with the ability to plan ahead.

How do I create a budget?

The 50/30/20 rule is an easy budgeting method that can help you to manage your money effectively, simply and sustainably.

The basic rule of thumb is to divide your monthly after-tax income into three spending categories: 50% for needs, 30% for wants and 20% for savings or paying off debt.

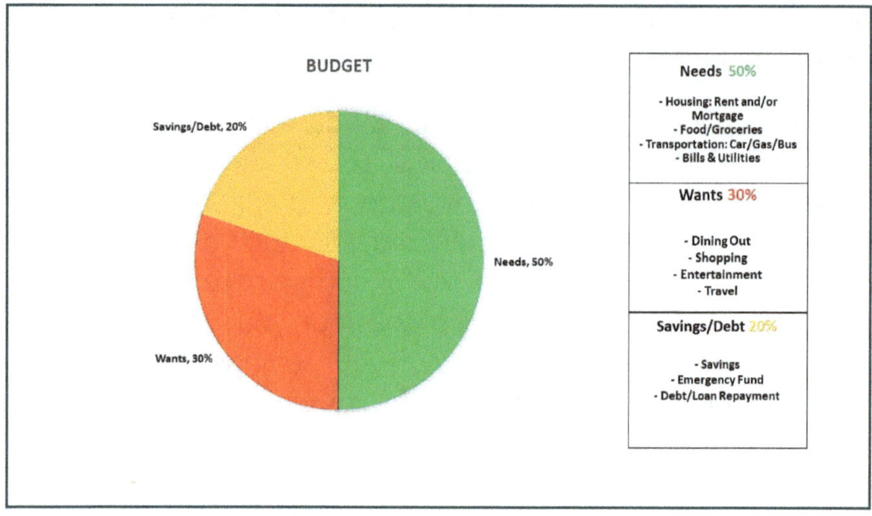

Tool Tip!: Nerdwallet.com has an online budget tool for your use here .

Wrapping Up!

Now that we have briefly covered some key Financial Literacy knowledge, I want to finalize by relaying a few key takeaways before moving to Step 2!

1. The first key to generational wealth is really setting this as a goal for yourself and your family. The secret here is to make this a part of your everyday life. You don't have to

obsess over it, but once you have the fundamentals down, the keys will start to open doors for you automatically. Just keep following on the path and if you fall, get back up and start at it again.

2. Your first goal along the generational wealth path is to increase your assets and reduce your liabilities. Carve out a plan to identify your liabilities (loans, credit card debt, etc.) and start to eliminate them, but remember to also prioritize saving. Remember, Debt should be no more than 20% of your monthly budget and Saving should be no less than 20%. The quicker you pay down your debt, the faster that 20% can all be allocated towards your savings.

3. Automate your savings! Once you have your debt under control ensure that you are saving at least 20% of your monthly income (after taxes). This can be done via direct deposit into your "High Yield" savings or checking accounts or in cash. Make sure you designate a plan for your savings as well. Make sure that every dollar saved has a function whether that be an Emergency Fund, Down Payment, Vacation or General Savings.

4. Last but not least, develop and stick to a monthly budget. The most common plan is 50/30/20 – 50% of your monthly income after taxes should be allocated towards NEEDS. 30% towards WANTS and 20% towards Debt/Saving. There are others that you may feel work better for you and your family, so research is key here. But if all else fails, those recommended here are tried and true.

2. Build a Team That Helps You Grow Your Wealth

This is another vital step one should consider when starting a generational wealth plan. You not only need a plan, but a team that helps you along the way. Your financial plan needs to be adaptable as you age. And you need to consider children, marriage, divorce, retirement and caring for aging parents. This can be a lot to try and manage on your own. That is where Financial Professionals step in to help.

As your wealth grows, there will be tax implications and estate planning concerns you'll want to address. So, you have to be prepared for it when comes your way. At some point, you will need to talk to a financial advisor, accountant or an estate attorney to ensure your financial plan and investments adapt as your life changes.

To find a financial advisor or planner, NAPFA (National Association of Personal Financial Advisors), and FPA (Financial Planning Association) are good places to start your search for help.

They will help you locate a planner in your area and always hire a fiduciary, who will act in your best interest.

Regardless of where you are in your life, the important thing is to start now. Just like weight loss doesn't happen overnight, neither does creation of generational wealth.

Creating generational wealth is the product of persistence and consistently reviewing your financial plan to see what's working and what may need to be adjusted.

Not all financial professionals are considered e qual and not all financial professionals may be needed in your specific case. To understand who you may want apart of your team. Lets take a look at the different types of financial planners and why they are normally used:

Financial Advisor

This is a professional who will help you manager your money. They do this by helping you make decisions related to investments, estate and tax planning and insurance. Always make sure that the advisor your chose holds a Financial Industry Regulatory Authority (FINRA) Series 65 license, which is **required** for them to be considered a professional public advisor. If they don't, I would suggest looking elsewhere.

Financial Planner

This is a professional who helps individuals and organizations create strategies to meet the long-term financial goals. They assist with budgeting and saving, investing and retirement planning. The often work for banks, wealth management firms, non-profits and can hold individual practices. Anyone, can call themselves a financial planner, however you will want to make sure you choose a planner that is licensed as a Certified Financial Planner (CFP), Chartered Financial Analyst (CFA), Chartered Financial Consultant (ChFC) or Certified Investment Management Analyst (CIMA). There are other designations but there are the most common licenses that prove that these individuals have met rigorous requirements to prove their credibility.

Each professional will charge a different fee so ensure that those costs fit within your budget. As a good rule of thumb, always do in-depth research before you trust ANYONE with your finances. If it sounds to good to be true, most often it is.

Tool Tip! CFP is a website you can use to verify a Certified Financial Planners certification status, Disciplinary history and any 10-year Bankruptcy Disclosures.

There are also digital platforms and programs that serve as Financial Planners called Robo-advisors.

Most Robo-advisors are FINRA members and use surveys to generate data about you, your current financial situation and future financial goals and develop algorithms or "logic" to relay advice and automatically complete investments on your behalf. This is all done with computers and programs and there is very little to no human interaction.

Some prefer this approach as the accounts are easy to setup online or via an app on your phone, they have a wide range of goal plans available and often times combine the ability to manage your individual account services with your investment portfolio as well. They even often include additional services such as financial literacy and investment education all in one platform. Another advantage of robo-advisors is that they are accessible at any time of the day or night, have low fees and opening balances.

I personally utilize a Financial Planner and meet with them quarterly to go over my goals, progress and any setback experienced the previous quarter. Together we develop a plan to move forward and re-asses if I am still on target, what I may need to do to get back on target or if I need to amend a target all together. I find the experience really empowering as I don't feel like I'm on the path alone. It takes some of the stress off, because the plans developed allow me to focus on measurable goals each quarter and as long as I am meeting those goals, I know I am on the right path.

Whichever professionals you choose to work with, know that they are on your "Team"! Working with them will help you achieve success and if you feel uncomfortable with something they are recommending, ask questions for clarification, but most importantly don't be afraid to push back or say no. At the end of the day, this is your Path to generational wealth for you and your family. This is your vision, always make whatever decisions you feel necessary to making sure that vision is realized and protect it at all costs!

Tool Tip!: *BrokerCheck by FINRA is a great tool to check Financial Professional registrations, securities licenses, complaints and employment history.*

3. Set Up a Trust Fund.

A trust fund is a way you can protect and dictate how your family receives your assets. You can set up a trustee who carries out your wishes, whether or not you're still alive. While you are living you can serve as the trustee to continue to manage your assets as you see fit. Your family would have access to your assets preceding your death and with the trust it will make it easier for them to continue building generational wealth. One of the main benefits of setting up a trust is that after your death, your family will be able to receive your assets a lot quicker than with a will due to not having to go through the probate process.

Another benefit of trusts is that you can avoid public records. This helps you protect your family's wealth by keeping transfers of assets private. If your trust meets certain conditions, it can also shield your assets (along with their appreciation) from estate tax after you are deceased. This translates into ensuring more money stays within your family, giving them more of a nest egg to work with during their lifetime.

A trust also outlines specific terms that your beneficiaries must meet and follow prior to being able to receive your assets. For instance, your trust may say that your grandchildren will receive inheritances from your assets in trust after they complete their college education or in increments over their lifetimes. This can ensure that your beneficiaries either pursue a higher education or don't burn through the assets you leave them all at once. This can put your family in a much better position for growing and passing down generational wealth prior to even receiving any inheritance.

In short, a trust allows you to be in the driver's seat with a plan, even when you're no longer physically present to make the decisions. Keep in mind that you don't have to have a certain amount of wealth to set up a trust, all you need to have are assets that you would like to pass down such as a home, bank account or life insurance. As your income and assets continue to grow, you can add them to your trust at any time.

There are several types of trusts available, and their individual benefits can vary, for now I will only focus on Living Trusts or Revocable Trusts.

What is a Living Trust (Revocable Trust) Fund?

This is a trust that can only be put in place while you are still living and able to make sound decisions related to the assets placed within it. This type of trust can be amended at any time while you are living and assets can be added to or taken out of it as you see fit.

How do I open a Trust Fund?

There are various ways to open a trust and availability can vary depending on the state you reside in. Please research your states laws related to trust formation to ensure you are covered appropriately. The most common methods for formation are online or through an estate planning attorney. I chose online via LegalZoom.com, however there are various online vendors that you can choose from and again their availability may be limited to state and federal laws based on your residence. I also chose to consult with an estate planning attorney before executing my trust to ensure that the setup I had completed was of benefit for me and would best position myself and my family for maintaining generational wealth through protecting my assets and ensuring that my assets were organized for my trustees and beneficiaries for generations to come.

I also own a business, can I add those assets to a Trust?

Yes! If your business is in the form of a Limited Liability Company (LLC), Limited Liability Partnership (LLP) or other business incorporation, placing your ownership shares in a Trust can protect your family members from debt obligations your business has incurred after your death. In the case where you are unable to tend to your affairs due to an unforeseen incapacitation, your family is able to continue running your business as outlined in your trust as well.

Through the creation of your trust you can take control of your assets and determine who they will be passed down to after your death and how those assets will be distributed to your family. This a pivotal part of your generational wealth creation plan and is intricate in ensuring that what you have worked hard for today can give your descendants a better future for tomorrow.

Summary

To setup a Living Trust (Revocable Trust) follow these steps:

1. Choose whether to make an individual or shared trust.

2. Decide what property to include in the trust.

3. Choose a <u>successor trustee</u> (you will be the current trustee while living.)

4. Decide who will be the trust's beneficiaries—that is, who will get the trust property. (Remember to set the Trust as the beneficiary of your life insurance policy.)

5. Create the trust document. You can get help from an attorney or use another vendor such as Legal Zoom.

6. Sign the document in front of a notary public.

7. Change the title of any trust property that has a title document—such as your house or car—to reflect that you now own the property as trustee of the trust.

4. Develop Multiple Revenue Streams.

Employment income is one source of revenue, but you may need to pull from multiple to create generational wealth. That's why it helps to develop multiple revenue streams.

The goal is to generate as much passive income as possible. Passive income doesn't require as much labor as active income from a job.

One way you can do this is through owning a globally diversified portfolio of stocks and bonds that yield dividends or pay interest. That is a passive revenue stream. You could also own real estate that is professionally managed to generate returns through appreciation or rental cash flow.

Starting a side hustle can also be another stream of income. If there's something you're passionate about that serves people or solves a problem, put those skills to work and charge for them. Plus, consider alternative ways to utilize your talents. Do you know someone who could benefit from your skills in a freelance capacity? Maybe you love photography and can start charging to shoot on the weekends. The beauty of having a side hustle is that you set the terms. You set your hours and you determine how much your time is worth.

In short, the more revenue streams you have, the larger your pool of wealth. Which means more money you can pass down to your family. If your descendants own those revenue streams, they'll have a steady supply of income to cover their living expenses and investment needs. They would just need to maintain those streams while developing additional streams of their own to pass down to the next generation to follow.

Keep in mind, one revenue stream can always lead to another. So, don't lose hope if you currently have only one stream. If you need help locating your next stream, a financial expert can help you find one that suits you. The earlier you start, the better.

5. Start a Business You Can Pass Down.

A business is an asset you can transfer to your children. If you decide to start one, make sure you offer a product or service people will always want. Take the same approach as Warren Buffett when he invested in Coca-Cola. Buffett chose Coca-Cola because of its long history of being an American staple. He felt confident that people will still want a Coke 100 years from now. Likewise, you want to build a business that pulls in customers 100 years from now.

6. Invest wisely and seek professional support

With so many investing options out there, you may not know where to start. You could deposit your money into a bank account, but doing so exposes it to inflation. The problem with inflation is that it steadily eats away at your money's value and that's a detriment to creating generational wealth.

Instead, you could put that money to work by investing it in the investment vehicles that historically beat inflation like stocks, bonds, real estate, or private equity. These assets grow your net worth and add to your passive income every year.

But what do you do if you don't have the time to pour through investment books? You could hire a financial expert. As previously covered a financial expert can inform you of investment opportunities that may fit your current situation.

7. Take Advantage of Legacy Wealth Planning

The chains of habit are too light to be felt until they are too heavy to be broken. You need to develop the right wealth-building habits. Habits that can financially free you and your family. Habits you can pass down to your children, who can then pass those habits down to theirs

Some legacy planning professionals will help show you how to protect your money from those looking to seize it. That way, you can rest easy, knowing your money is safely protected. You'll have a clear mind focused on creating generational wealth.

8. Purchase Life Insurance

Life Insurance is a #1 must have when creating generational wealth. As a constant I will go so far as to say that without Life Insurance, ones plan to creating generational wealth is severely lacking. No matter what age you may be along your journey, life insurance is pivotal. The younger you are the more important this component of the generational wealth building plan is to you, so lets get to it!

Life insurance allows the policyholder a cash benefit that their family can utilize to take care of their final wishes such as funeral and burial expenses. Life insurance also allows your family the ability to pay off any debts that you may have acquired prior to you transition such as a mortgage, vehicle loan, student loan or medical related debt. Aside from these all remaining funds are paid to beneficiaries directly after any probate process is concluded on the estate. Now, if you have followed the plan, all life insurance proceeds will be paid directly to your Trust, that you should have set as your life insurance beneficiary according Step #3 above, and proceed payment will bypass the probate process and remain out of reach of creditors.

HOWEVER THAT IS NOT ALL LIFE INSURANCE CAN DO TO CREATE GENERATIONAL WEALTH!

Life Insurance is one of the secret keys that the wealthy utilize to generate wealth while they are living as well. If, I told you that life insurance can allow you to passively grow your wealth, free from IRS taxation. If I told you that life insurance could allow you access to capital to fund your business, purchase real estate or give yourself a low interest loan without needing to go through a bank or credit union, or supplement your early retirement plan. What would you do? Would you call me crazy?

WELL HELLO, CALL ME CRAZY!

Life Insurance allows you the power to do all of those things. Lets get into how.....!!There are various types of Life Insurance that you can choose from for your plan. A lot of you have already heard of Term Life Insurance, but many have not heard of Permanent or Variable Life Insurance. These two types of Insurance are the ones I want you to focus on during your path to creating generational wealth.

What is Term Life Insurance?

Term Life Insurance is a Life Insurance – supplement that as of late has been promoted and pushed as an overall Life Insurance strategy for people of all ages, due to its High Policy Limit to Low Cost Ratio. One can easily obtain $100,000-

$500,000 worth of insurance for under $50/month. This is usually the type of policy that is offered to you through your employer but also the type that you can purchase outside of work as well. This policy is great, but as I previously mentioned as a supplement to Permanent/Variable Life Insurance which we will discuss next. Term life Insurance to me is a kin to renting an apartment. You pay premiums for the policy value selected every month usually for a specified term (10, 20 or 30 years). If you live to term say 10 years then your policy value does not pay out and the premiums you paid into the policy for that term are not returned. You would then have to renew your term or take out another policy if you want to continue coverage, but this is usually at your 'attained age' which most often than not results in a high payment per month at that point. For example, maybe you are a 30-year old male taking out a 20 year $250,000 Term Policy for $30/month. You would pay that premium for 20 years resulting in a total cost of $7200. If you don't die during that period, at age 50, you can renew your policy for an additional 20-year term but the cost would now be $80/month or $19,200. That increase in cost is a liability, the monthly cost is technically a liability as it results in no usable asset while you are living.

What is Permanent Life Insurance?

Permanent (or Whole) Life insurance is similar to Term Life insurance in that it is Insurance on ones Life in which you pay a set monthly premium for specified selected benefit payable upon your death. However, the unique characteristic that sets Permanent Life Insurance apart from Term Insurance is that the death benefit builds cash value for you while you are alive. This is done for you automatically via the Insurance Company investing of a portion of your premiums and other policyholders premiums in funds that are consider stable and safe under normal market conditions. As you age and continue to pay your premiums your policy gains cash value either through dividend payments directly to your policies cash value fund or through interest payments often in excess of 4-5% per year. As your cash value increases on your policy and is added in addition to your death benefit, increasing any future payout or is available to you to withdraw of borrow against (at a much lower interest rate as a ban loan) as needed without affecting your baseline policy benefit. You can either keep the cash and not pay it back to your accumulated cash value or essentially make a lump sum or additional monthly payment to pay your self back. Often times if you do not pay the cash value accumulation back to your policy upon your death there is no penalty and you baseline benefit selection will still apply and be payable upon your death.

Another great benefit of these policies also is that premiums can be paid monthly for the duration of your life (with associated cash value continuing to build for you as well) or you can select a specific pay-up period for your policy as well such as 20 or 30 years. What this means is that you pay a monthly premium for a set 20 or 30 years and then after that period you no longer have to pay any additional premiums for the duration of your life. Your policy benefit will remain in place, guaranteed and your cash value will continue to accumulate and grow at the rate specified as well. Hence the name Permanent, you now fully own this policy an asset.

For example:

Per the policy value illustration below, for a 33 year-old male with a $250,000 Permanent Life Insurance Policy you would pay about $247/month or $2962 per year. As you can see at the end of year 5, he would have a guaranteed $250,000 death benefit, but would also have accumulated a Guaranteed Cash value of $5,773 that he can borrow against. This man, will have made over $1,154 dollars, per year, simply by paying his insurance premiums and still have a ¼ million dollar death benefit, forbid anything happen to him during that 5 year period.

Look at year 10, same yearly premium, but now he has $19,378 cash benefit (asset) available to borrow against or withdraw. That **asset** is almost a 20% down payment on a $100,000 investment property that will also turn around and generate **additional cash flow** and asset accumulation. That asset can then be handed down to your children, as it is included in the trust you created above, which is also a beneficiary of the additional $250,000 Life Insurance Benefit on this policy as well. **Do you see that, that is 3 assets added to your generational wealth from just $247/month.**

End of Year	Age	Guaranteed			Non-Guaranteed Midpoint			Non-Guaranteed Current		
		Yearly Guaranteed Premium	Cash Surrender Value	Death Benefit (BOY)	Premium Outlay	Cash Surrender Value	Death Benefit (BOY)	Premium Outlay	Cash Surrender Value	Death Benefit (BOY)
5	38	2,962	5,773	250,000	2,962	6,362	251,884	2,962	6,961	253,780
10	43	2,962	19,378	250,000	2,962	21,789	258,050	2,962	24,318	266,432
20	53	2,962	48,555	250,000	2,962	59,438	279,116	2,962	71,557	311,356
37	70	2,875	119,358	250,000	2,875	168,438	331,663	2,875	229,586	432,687
52	85&	2,875	189,128	250,000	2,875	312,415	398,801	2,875	483,666	604,143
62	95	2,875	221,235	250,000	2,875	413,721	456,012	2,875	697,209	757,836

Now do you see the "Non-guaranteed Midpoint" and "Non-Guaranteed Current "columns? What these illustrations are showing are related to the market conditions that can arise and increase your cash value accumulation based upon the "better than expected" investment portfolio performance that your premiums are being invested into. Though these cash value accumulations are not guaranteed they can give you a really good look into what your cash value growth can look like if the market continues to perform well. As you can see the growth there is even better!

What is Variable Life Insurance?

Variable Life Insurance another type of Permanent (Whole) Life Insurance as we talked about previously, but with a few additional features that may appeal to you specifically. Variable life insurance gives you greater flexibility when it comes to your premium payments and death benefits. With variable life insurance the premiums you pay can be made at any time and in any amount. So if you are having a rough patch due to a job loss or illness. You can keep your policy in place but pay less than illustrated premium for that period. You can then catch up on the difference at a later time once things smooth out, however, the cash value will not have accumulated as illustrated due to the reduced payment period not being placed into sub accounts as originally intended to result in the growth over that period.

With Universal life you can also increase your death benefit by making lump-sum payments into your policy which will increase the cash value but also be added on top of your death benefit should something happen to you after that period.

The caveat with universal life is that the premiums are paid through the policies cash value, therefore if you do not have enough cash value to pay your premiums at the end of the year, the policy will lapse. Also, because the premiums are being saved and placed into sub accounts vs direct investments, the premiums tend to be higher than with whole life and they increase every single year versus remaining constant as with whole life.

Due to this fact, it is often noted with variable life that as you age the cost begins to get so high that the cash value accumulation begins to decrease down to zero as the premiums (paid from the cash value) being eating away at what has been accumulated due to the cost rising exponentially.

For this reason, I personally prefer Whole life Insurance over Variable Life Insurance as the risk outweighs the benefits. For creation of generational wealth, I appreciate the guarantees that Whole Life Presents. It gives me a greater peace of mind know what will be and how I can utilize those guarantees to elevate my family.

TYPES OF GENERATIONAL WEALTH

Launching a Family business

How to move from business idea to launch?

Once you've done it a couple of times, starting a new venture becomes much easier and more streamlined. A lot of mistakes are made in the process by early entrepreneurs. Most aren't deadly, but they can prove to be very expensive later on. These eleven tips to launch your business will help you skip the pitfalls and start on a better foundation.

Pursuing entrepreneurship can be risky, with 45% of businesses failing in the first 5 years, but for most of us, entrepreneurship is the best opportunity we have to change the trajectory of our lives and impact our families for generations. Creating a business plan is essential to count the cost, weigh your options, and ultimately prepare you for the journey of starting your business.

Your business or product launch is the first impression people will remember. It's not enough to create a great business or product. If you want to be successful, you need to take steps to plan and execute a well-timed, memorable launch that will bring your product to the attention of more people in more locations. In today's competitive marketplace, businesses need to begin their promotional efforts before they actually start selling their products or offerings. Additionally, companies need to find ways to stand out from the noise while making the right first impression on early adopters. These steps can help you make your launch a success.

Steps for launching a new product in a way that's smart, strategic, and most of all effective:

Find & Know Your Why

1. Why are you doing this?

2. Why are you planning to do it this way?

Dig deep. Own it. Be able to convey it clearly, quickly and passionately to others. After finding and knowing your business plan determine whether the idea might be successful. It's important to,

3. Consider who your customers are and

4. How your product or service compares to your competitors. After that, you can consider,

5. Where you are going to get your funds and

6. How you will use them. Equally important is your growth strategy, figuring out

7. How you will get business and how much it will cost to acquire a single customer.

Start Building a Community

You can't make your dreams a reality if you can't find the people. Don't wait till your doors are open to start trying to find your customers, and then immediately have to hard sell them to keep the doors open. Start curating your community today. Then you'll open with an existing audience you have relationships with and have trust with. Start identifying who you need and securing them. As the saying goes, "if you want to go fast, go alone. If you want to go further, go together." Along the way they'll teach you a lot and help you get the product and marketing right the first time.

Business Planning

The next thing to consider is a business plan. The business plan is meant to help you determine how well your idea satisfies all areas. If you have tons of capital and a great product then you can add to your team by hire, but if you don't have the capital or the capacity then it doesn't matter how good your idea is until you can devise a plan to overcome those obstacles.

You don't necessarily need a full-fledged, fat stack of paper business plan to start. Things move fast today, they will inevitably change multiple times along the way, and certainly when you raise funding. Do go through the process of answering all of the questions a business plan requires. It will make sure you aren't forgetting things. Too many entrepreneurs and business ideas with potential have been lost by those taking many months and years to create a business plan which is ultimately useless.

Some of the first things you really want to focus on here is an executive summary, a plan for the initial marketing you will test, and some information on your financials. Especially cash flow projections for the next 3-5 years. Again, most of all new business fail within the first five years, if you have a solid plan to get you through that period, you will be better set up for continued success. Additionally, you'll want to create a pitch deck. For a winning deck, take a look at the pitch deck template created by Silicon Valley legend, Peter Thiel. You can make use of The Cultivate Launch Track which is a free program designed to help you through the business planning process.

Tool Tip: When creating business plans I like to utilize online platform **LivePlan.** They have tons of business plan templates across various business segments and they help you develop a solid plan step-by-step.

Start Testing & Get Feedback

By now you've had plenty of contact with plenty of people. Start testing the waters. Just because you've created an ingenious product that (you believe) fills an existing gap in the marketplace doesn't mean you're ready to start selling. Savvy business owners take time to test their new items and perform necessary adjustments. Before listing a product for sale on your website, or stocking it in your retail store, collect feedback from surveys and focus groups so you can make any needed improvements before releasing the product wide. A good tool for this is through Social Media, if you've taken the time to build a solid following, then test your products appeal via that following. If their feedback is positive, that will build a great buzz in want for the product once it goes to market. This following most often turn out to be immediate buyers also.

One of the reasons that testing is so crucial is that it ensures a product's first impression with buyers will be a positive one.

Business Structure

By this point you know you are going through with building this business. You are committed. You know who your initial founding team is. You know why you are building it and in turn what type of structure you need for that culture and desired exit.

The best step is filing an LLC and obtaining a tax ID number. This can be done online in less than an hour. However, if you plan to raise funding and really do anything sizable with this venture, invest in a good attorney to ask the right questions, get the paperwork right and structure shares and voting rights in the best way for your future plans (and in case they fall apart). In the event you are looking to raise significant financing a C-Corp in Delaware might be the way to go as that tends to be the desired structure by investors.

The best way that I have found to do this is through either LegalZoom or IncFile online. I have setup business through both of these online provides as the cost is affordable and the step-by-step process ensures that you are knowledgeable about what is available and what you need. They also have add-ons that allow you to obtain legal advice from an attorney at anytime regarding your business, future business plans or issues.

Just get moving! There will be lots of decisions to be made every day. You won't get them all right. What's important is that you keep moving forward. It's ideal if you have a consultant or someone who has been on all sides of this process (founder and funder) and been through it all to give you some feedback and guidance through the process. They can help you ask the right questions, watch out for what you don't know or help with networking.

Create a Schedule and Stick to It

It's easy to lose sight of your goals while trying to launch a new product. Smart business owners create detailed production schedules to ensure tasks are completed on time and team members are held accountable for their roles.

While it's important to ensure your schedule is realistic, entrepreneurs also need to consider the best times of year to release their new products. For example, depending on the item you're selling, you might want to consider seasonal factors or the timing of trade shows or pop culture events.

Identify Your Marketing Channels

Gone are the days when businesses could market their products on only one or two sales channels. Today, savvy startups maximize potential sales by targeting as many potential channels as possible. Along with traditional outlets like TV, radio, and mailers, modern businesses promote their goods on websites, social media pages, and online retail sites. They create email marketing campaigns, utilize PPC advertising and even contact customers via texts. The more channels you target with your marketing materials, the more opportunities you will have to find new and profitable audiences.

Investing in the Stock Market

Investing in stocks just means buying tiny shares of ownership in a public company. Those small shares are known as the company's stock, and by investing in it, you're committing that the company will grow and perform well over time. When that happens, your shares become more valuable, and other investors may be willing to buy them from you for more than you paid for them at a later date. That means you would then earn a profit once you decide to sell them.

How to invest in the stock market in six steps

- Decide how you want to invest in the stock market
- Choose an investing (brokerage) account
- Learn the difference between investing in stocks vs funds
- Set a budget for your stock market investment
- Focus on investing for the long-term
- Manage your investment portfolio

Should I invest in stocks, bonds or funds?

The answer to what you choose to invest in really comes down to three things: the time horizon for your goals, how much risk you're willing to take and what things are you already interested in. Let's tackle time horizon first: If you're investing for a far-off goal, like retirement, you should be invested primarily in stocks (equities). While there is some risk here, which we will discuss in greater detail later, the reward upside is generally much better than with bonds. Since you have more time, you will want to take advantage of that upside as much as you can. However, remember there is a potential for downside as well, but having time on your side gives you plenty of time to recover should that occur.

Investing in well performing equities will allow your money to grow and outpace inflation over time. As your goal gets closer, you can slowly start to dial back your equity allocation and add in more bonds, which are generally safer more stable investments and allow your gains to essentially begin to lock themselves in as you get closer to your goal.

The second factor is: Risk tolerance. The stock market goes up and down, and if you're prone to panicking when it does the latter, you're better off investing slightly more conservatively, with a lighter allocation towards equities (stocks). Additionally, if you are new to investing but don't have a large time horizon, you will want have what is termed a moderate risk tolerance. This will give you the most balanced investment mindset in that it will allow you to choose stocks that aren't particularly too risk but also are too conservative either. The returns wont be as high as with those that are high risk tolerance but downsides tend to be lower as well.

STOCK INVESTING TIPS

How do I choose my stocks?

- Determine your investing approach
- Decide how much you will invest in stocks
- Open in investment account
- Choose your stocks

Now that you have chosen your investing approach the next step is to essentially determine your investment budget.

This will take us back to your 50/30/20 budget plan created earlier. Investing will still be allocated to your 20% Debt/Saving portion of your budget. If you can allocate more than 20% that is great but remember to always seek a proper balance between debt payment and general savings. Also remember that investing is for the long-term, only invest funds that you will not immediately need. The goal is to allow you investment to grow over time so if you are going to need the funds you are using anywhere between 10-15 years from now, those are not funds you should be using for investing.

Next, we need to know how to open an investment account. This is fairly easy today via the options available. You can open an investment account online or via your mobile phone for free through Robinhood or Stash and even through Cash App. With that being said, not all investment accounts are created equal so research the best option for you. Some investment accounts have limited companies or funds that you can invest in. Online there are other accounts such as TD Ameritrade, Etrade, Charles Schwab and others.

Why You Should Invest in Stocks

1. You can start investing with as little as you want.

Nowadays, many brokerage firms allow clients to purchase fractional shares. This means you can invest based on dollar amounts instead of number of shares. For example, if Company ABC's stock price is $200 but you only have $100 to invest, you can purchase ½ a share of Company ABC.

2. Many low-cost/free brokerage firms.

Opening a brokerage account should be free, transferring funds in and out of your brokerage account is usually free, and, lastly, buying and selling shares should be free. If any of those are currently costing you money, you may want to consider finding a brokerage firm with better benefits. There are several to choose from such as Ameritrade, Robinhood, Stash, etc. Also, these brokerages often offer incentives such as free shares when you refer a friend or hit certain milestones with your account. If you don't feel comfortable with your knowledge, some of these brokerages also offer free training and educational tools for you also.

3. A large selection of investments to pick from.

There are thousands of individual stocks you can invest in. But for those who don't want to pick their own stocks for a variety of reasons, like not having time to research companies or lack the knowledge on how to determine if a company is good, investing in Exchange Traded Funds (ETF's) or Mutual Funds is also a solid option.

It Doesn't Take A Genius

What you do need is basic knowledge on how to get an account set up and which ETFs and/or mutual funds to park your money in for the next several decades. Investing in funds that track a known index such as the S&P 500, that is also low-cost is often a reasonable choice.

ETFs and Mutual Funds are Easy To Diversify

You should not put all your eggs in one basket. To overcome that, one can simply invest in ETFs and/or mutual funds, both of which resemble a basket of underlying companies. For example, if you invest in VTI (Vanguard Total Stock Market Index Fund), you automatically gain exposure to about 3,500 different companies!

Additionally, you can even gain exposure to real estate by investing in the stock market. A common way to do this is to invest in companies that build real estate (think Lennar or D.R. Horton) or companies that own and invest real estate. Some of these publicly-listed companies, called Real Estate Investment Trusts (REITs), are even required to pay a minimum of 90% of their taxable income as dividends to shareholders. REITs are often some of the highest dividend-payers out there. To further diversify your real estate exposure, not only can you invest in REITs, you can invest in an REIT mutual fund or ETF (like VNQ) to own a basket of REITs with a single investment.

Investment Strategies

If you are new to investing or don't have a lot of time to actively research individual stocks or funds to invest in. I recommend investing in ETF's or Mutual Funds. There are hundreds if not thousands to choose from but I want to give you a few easy strategies to use to guide you along the right path here.

Disclaimer: I am not a licensed financial advisor so please understand this is purely informational and you assume all risk and responsibility for the investments you make. I do recommend speaking with your licensed financial advisor before making any investments to ensure that whatever you invest in will work for you.

I myself have spent several years investing in the market and one of the inspirations for my investment philosophy is Warren Buffett. Warren Buffett is an extremely knowledgeable billionaire investor and philanthropist. You may not have heard of him but his company, Berkshire Hathaway, owns substantial shares of stock in various companies you have heard of such as Geico, Coca-Cola and Kraft Heinz. In 2014, he recommended what has come to be known as the "90/10 rule". What this rule is an ETF invested allocation of **90% equities and 10% bonds.** In 2017 he went a step further and specifically recommended one select **a low-cost S&P 500 ETF (Vanguard).**

Therefore the strategy in full would translate to **invest 90% of your funds there continuously and 10% in a low-cost Short Term Government Bond Fund.** This split has been tested and the results have shown that this mix has outperformed splits that are more conservative(weighted towards bonds), returns outperformed and losses were minimal.

I personally utilize this strategy with my portfolio has performed very well for me. It is simple to manage as I only have two funds to invest in, I only have to re-balance it once a year to ensure the allocations are maintained and my portfolio returns often beat the returns of those investing in individual stocks and managing their portfolio 24/7. The two funds I chose were **Vanguard 500 Index Fund ETF (VOO) – 90% and Vanguard Short-Term Treasury Index Fund ETF (VGSH) – 10%.** There are others, just ensure you expense ratios are below .05%.

Automatic Investing

Not a lot of people are aware of this amazing feature that many brokerage firms offer. Automatic investing is where you configure your brokerage account to withdraw a specified dollar amount from your bank account (or another brokerage account, if you want) on a fixed, monthly schedule and have those dollars automatically invested into a fund that you already own. For example, you can set up your automatic investment schedule to withdraw $500 from your checking account on the 1st of every month and invest it straight into the VOO and VGSH funds at the allocations you have already pre-set.

Additionally, by setting up automatic investing, you get the sweet benefit of dollar-cost averaging (DCA). DCA is an investment strategy where you invest your money over time instead of investing a lump sum all at once. Doing so theoretically reduces the volatility of stock market swings that are bound to happen.

Lastly, because you know your cash isn't just sitting around in a bank account earning less than 0.5% every year, it instead is automatically getting invested in the stock market, you can largely sit back and watch your net worth grow exponentially over time. You don't have to stress over stock market swings or worry about individual stocks collapsing after earnings reports because automatic investing socks away my money into only the funds you choose, automatically giving you diversification of your portfolio.

AN INTRODUCTION TO CRYPTO

What is crypto and how does it work?

Cryptocurrency (or "crypto") is a digital form of money that is considered a more secure medium of exchange. It can be used to buy goods and services, but uses an online ledger with strong cryptography to secure online transactions. Much of the interest in these unregulated currencies is to trade for profit with speculators, at times driving prices upward. The main point of cryptocurrency is to fix the problems of traditional currencies by putting the power and responsibility in the currency holders' hands.

Why You Should Care About Cryptocurrency/Advantages

The big idea is that because transactions are public, irreversible, mostly un-hackable and controlled by the people, users and their digital finances are more protected. Of course, many benefits come with cryptocurrency. Below are four key reasons why people have begun to care more about cryptocurrency of late.

1. Cryptocurrency Is Owned By Everyone

Cryptocurrency functions similarly to any traditional, national currency with a few fundamental differences.

Cryptocurrency does not stand for debt. It strictly represents itself, and its value is determined by what someone is willing to trade for it. The fact that cryptocurrency is decentralized plays an essential role in how its currency value is determined.

Nobody owns or regulates a cryptocurrency. Its value is not subject to a country's political whims or a central bank's monetary policy.

2. Cryptocurrency Is Almost Impossible to Forge

Cryptocurrency operates on a blockchain, which is the distributed ledger we talked about above. Understanding blockchain technology helps you understand why this is the key to the power of the digital currency. The "block" is composed of chunks of encrypted data. The "chain" is the public database in which the blocks are stored and sequentially related to each other. Every block in the blockchain has a specific code that distinguishes itself from all other blocks in existence. This unique code is called a hash. Blocks of information being added to a blockchain are added chronologically. A new block is added directly after the last block created, which also has its own unique hash.

3. Cryptocurrency Transactions Are (Mostly) Confidential

Cryptocurrency depends on well-designed math to track the exchange between two people or companies.

This occurs mostly anonymously. While the ledger or list of transactions is publicly viewable worldwide, the parties exchanging cryptocurrency are more private. By definition, cryptocurrencies are held electronically in digital wallets. The owner is the holder of the private key to the wallet. The currency is exchanged digitally from mostly anonymous wallets owned by the users.

4. Cryptocurrency Security Grows Through Time & Value

Earlier, we talked about how a hack or manipulation would require an enormous amount of power and money to the point that it would essentially become a worthless endeavor. To elaborate, a hacker would need to control over fifty percent of the computers making up the "consensus" network. The consensus network is simply all the computers that receive copies of the blockchain or distributed ledger. For more established cryptos like Bitcoin or Ethereum, the cryptocurrency networks are so big that a hack undertaking is mostly impossible.

Cryptocurrency is a form of payment that can be exchanged online for goods and services. Many companies have issued their own currencies, often called tokens, and these can be traded specifically for the good or service that the company provides. Think of them as you would arcade tokens or casino chips. You'll need to exchange real currency for the cryptocurrency to access the good or service. There are also crypto ATM's now in existence. Here the individual owners of cryptocoins can utilize their wallets keys to convert certain cryptocoins into cash and withdraw it from these crypto ATMs.

Best cryptocurrencies by market capitalization

These are the 10 largest trading cryptocurrencies by market capitalization as tracked by Coin-Market-Cap, a cryptocurrency data and analytics provider.

These include, Bitcoin, Ethereum, Binancecoin, Tether, Solana, Cardano, XRP, USD coin, Polka dot, Dogecoin. If you are planning to invest in crypto these mentioned currencies are the ones to consider. I myself own crypto through the Robinhood

Platform, however I move to make sure that my overall portfolio allocation towards crypto is no more than 5%. Crypto is still a fairly new investment class, therefore it is highly volatile. As my goal is to create generational wealth, I want to ensure that I have exposure to this market but that I am not overly leveraged in this emerging market as to take a huge financial hit if my investment does not perform as well as I had hoped.

Why are cryptocurrencies so popular?

Cryptocurrencies appeal to their supporters for a variety of reasons. Here are some of the most popular

- Supporters see cryptocurrencies such as bitcoin as the currency of the future and are racing to buy them now, presumably before they become more valuable
- Some supporters like the fact that cryptocurrency removes central banks from managing the money supply, since over time these banks tend to reduce the value of money via inflation
- Other supporters like the technology behind cryptocurrencies, the blockchain, because it's a decentralized processing and recording system and can be more secure than traditional payment systems
- Some speculators like cryptocurrencies because they're going up in value and have no interest in the currencies' long-term acceptance as a way to move money

5. How do I buy cryptocurrency?

While some cryptocurrencies, including bitcoin, are available for purchase with U.S. dollars, others require that you pay with bitcoins or another cryptocurrency. To buy cryptocurrencies, you'll need a "wallet," an online app that can hold your currency. Generally, you create an account on an exchange (like Robinhood, Coinbase or Crypto.com), and then you can transfer real money to buy cryptocurrencies such as bitcoin or Ethereum. Coinbase is one popular cryptocurrency trading exchange where you can create both a wallet and buy and sell bitcoin and other cryptocurrencies. Also, a growing number of online brokers offer cryptocurrencies, such as eToro, Tradestation, Crypto.com and Robinhood.

6. Are cryptocurrencies legal?

There's no question that they're legal in the United States, though China has essentially banned their use, and ultimately whether they're legal depends on each individual country.

7. How do I protect myself?

If you're looking to buy a cryptocurrency in an ICO, read the fine print in the company's prospectus for this information:

- Who owns the company? An identifiable and well-known owner is a positive sign.
- Are there other major investors who are investing in it? It's a good sign if other well-known investors want a piece of the currency.
- Will you own a stake in the company or just currency or tokens? This distinction is important. Owning a stake means you get to participate in its earnings (you're an owner), while buying tokens simply means you're entitled to use them, like chips in a casino.
- Is the currency already developed, or is the company looking to raise money to develop it? The further along the product, the less risky it is.

It can take a lot of work to comb through a prospectus; the

more detail it has, the better your chances it's legitimate. But even legitimacy doesn't mean the currency will succeed. That's an entirely separate question, and that requires a lot of market savvy. Again, whatever you do ensure that your at this time your exposure does not exceed 5% of your overall portfolio value.

AN INTRODUCTION TO REAL ESTATE

Why Real Estate Is The One Asset That Will Always Build Generational Wealth

Real estate is a pretty unique asset class with a range of underlying characteristics and strategies that can serve multiple purposes for an investor. To understand the attraction to this particular asset, here are a few of its multifaceted advantages.

Passivity

Passive real estate investments don't require a full-time commitment and leave the headaches to someone else. The passive nature of real estate also allows investors to leverage their capital across multiple assets to generate multiple streams of income instead of sinking all of their assets into a single asset.

Easily Transferable

Real estate is easily transferable to succeeding generations. The wealthy set up trusts to hold their real estate assets, and upon the death of the grantor, ownership automatically transfers through the trust. Real estate conveyances at death are much less complicated than conveyances of business disagreements that may arise in roles, compensation, contributions, distributions, etc.

THE BEST RETURN O N IN V ESTMEN T

When you are thinking about saving money, you naturally look for the solution that will provide you with the best return on your money. You want the highest interest rate. But when you compare what a bank is willing to give you for your investment and what you will earn if you invest in real estate, there is really no comparison.

Banks often offer a lower percentage at best. However, a real estate investment can actually double overtime. And real estate is not likely to devalue in the same manner as most investments.

Stable income

Real estate is one of the few investment opportunities that will provide you with a sizable and steady income. Multifamily rental properties provide owners with rental income each month that cover the property's cost and return a profit. And as the property value increases, so with the amount of rent that you will be earning from your tenants. This is the perfect way to create a guaranteed income for your children as they grow into adults and begin to provide for the next generation of your family.

Illiquid

Because real estate is illiquid, it's insulated from mob mentality and broader market volatility because it cannot be easily disposed of. Investors in passive investment vehicles typically lock up their capital for long periods of typically at least five years. Illiquidity protects investors from themselves and prevents them from making snap decisions in a fleeting moment of panic they might regret later.

Most often humans are easily tempted. And when you have your money in a savings account, in stocks or other very liquid investments, it is easy to turn those savings into cash. And unfortunately, that cash is all too often spent in a wasteful manner. However, real estate is not something that you can quickly and easily turn into cash on a whim. Instead, you need to go through a somewhat lengthy process to convert it to cash. That time is a safety feature that keeps many real estate investors from wasting their hard-earned money on something consumable or that will lose value.

Sustainability and Predictability

Real estate is a proven commodity. There may be down years, but in the long term, real estate constantly appreciates and cash flowing real estate generates consistent income. Trends come and go in other industries and sectors, but real estate continues to be consistent.

Real estate isn't the only asset capable of creating generational wealth that grows over time, but it is often found in the portfolios of those recognizable names like Rockefeller. Although real estate values can fluctuate from time to time, over the long haul, real estate has consistently appreciated over time from inflation and its intrinsic value.

Generational wealth is about creating long-term financial security for your family. By investing in real estate, you will be growing your money more rapidly, securely, and safely than you could with any other investment type. And that will provide for your immediate financial needs as well as the needs of future generations.

4 Tips for Building Generational Wealth

Through Real Estate

Offset low interest rates

Because of the cashflow nature of real estate, where long-term leases can enable stable occupancy that drives income yield, clients can find stability with real estate to complement other parts of their portfolios, The right vehicle can depend on a client's risk tolerance and investment goals; while some investors with an active approach may want to directly own property, there are also a number of more passive options, including private real estate funds and traded or non-traded real estate investment trusts (REITs), which provide similar benefits for those who don't want to actively manage a physical property.

Hedge against inflation

With inflation expected to rise in the U.S., investors are seeking strategies to offset that risk in their portfolio. Historically, REITs have performed better than the broader equity market during periods of moderate or high inflation, making them an effective hedge, says Tim Barker, Managing Director at BNY Mellon Wealth Management.

Due to the embedded characteristics of the asset class, rents typically rise in line with inflation measures, real estate income during the last 25 years has increased at a slightly higher level than inflation.

This differs from fixed-income investments, which are tied to interest rates and don't offer the same inflationary protection.

Adjust your exposure

Investors new to real estate opportunities don't necessarily need to recalibrate their portfolio extensively to expose themselves to the benefits of the sector. Growth investing is not going away as long as interest rates remain low, but for many of our higher-net- worth clients, exposure of around 5-7% of a portfolio in real estate, including liquid REITs and illiquid real estate investments, would be appropriate.

Consider gifting strategies

Real estate is also a flexible option for gifting, allowing for appreciation while also giving the current owner of the asset liquidity during their lifetime. A vacation home, for example, can be a meaningful gift that has both sentimental and financial value for future generations. Investing directly in other types of property can also be a vehicle for wealth growth and transfer, while avoiding estate tax headaches.

The lower valuations of the minority interests in the assets create future tax savings for the estate owner. The same valuation discounts at death are available for the original owner who retains only a minority interest in the real estate. That said, real estate can also be complicated to navigate within an estate plan, and it can be helpful to work with an estate planning strategist to ensure that real estate is transferred as tax-efficiently as possible.

OBSTACLES TO CREATING GENERATIONAL WEALTH

A Pew Research study showed that "incomes of first-generation college graduates lag those of other graduates."

The income lag, coupled with student loan debt, are obstacles to homeownership and wealth creation.

The wealth gap exists in America. Pay inequality, institutional racism, housing segregation and redlining all continue to create barriers that disparately impact Black and Hispanic communities' ability to generate wealth via homeownership.

A study by Life Happens and LIMRA showed that although African Americans are more insured than any other group, they are underinsured, meaning they don't have enough life insurance to act as a replacement for income, debt, or to build wealth.

Unfortunately, the default for parents is to work hard and pass down assets. But, that scenario is unlikely to work in most cases. That's why an estimated 70% of generational wealth doesn't make it past the second generation, and 90% disappears by the third.

Most parents who started from humble beginnings don't want their children to experience the same struggles as they did grow up. But finding the right balance is a challenge. Building wealth that survives more than one generation requires more than financial assets.

Do you want to leave a lasting legacy that spans generations to come? If yes and while this is a noble goal to have, you should not underestimate the unique challenges that come with leaving behind generational wealth. Today we're going to talk about the top 5 financial planning challenges of generational wealth, and what you can do to combat them. If these challenges are left unaddressed, they may become major obstacles to investing for generational wealth.

Maintaining Wealth for More Than Three Generations

SETTING UP GENERATIONS TO ENJOY WEALTH FOR YEARS TO COME

Having open lines of Communication plays a major role in maintaining wealth for more than three generations. Open communication builds the trust that is the basis for sustaining your family's wealth.

Preparing the next generation for what they can expect is critical and you should take advantage of any teachable moments that arise. By doing this, the next generation can learn, understand and eventually participate in decisions that can affect the family's wealth. It could also be a good idea to introduce a wealth expert/advisor to help facilitate a productive discussion. This could lead to a better understanding among the family members and help them discover shared values and passions. These values and passions could result in the members to work together and share in decision-making regarding the family wealth. They are also critical in helping them stay together during times of adversity.

Have you heard the old proverb

"Shirtsleeves to shirtsleeves in three generation"

It's an idea that most generational wealth doesn't make it past the third generation. In most cases, it looks like the below...

The first generation grows up poor and works diligently to create wealth. The second generation saw their parents' work ethic and struggles, so they appreciate and protect the wealth that's passed on to them. The third generation, however, never witnessed firsthand the hard work and sacrifices their grandparents made to build their wealth. As a result, they don't appreciate the wealth they receive, and they squander it.

It's difficult to plan for a generational shift that may not happen for another 20 or 30 years, but there are systems you can put in place to prevent it from happening. Which leads us to challenge #2.

Focusing On The Right Threats To Wealth

Many wealthy individuals assume the market and economy are biggest threats to the preservation of their wealth—but this is far from the truth. Most often, the biggest threat to generational wealth is a lack of communication.

As we discussed above, most generational wealth doesn't make it past the third generation. We've all been taught to not talk about money sometimes even within our own family. But if you're not communicating with your loved ones about your assets, they may not know how to manage them once you're gone.

The key to mitigating this threat is to openly communicate with your family about the following:

Tell stories and share about the struggles the previous generations went through to create wealth. It is important to instill a strong sense of appreciation and work ethic in the younger generation. What you want to communicate is that wealth is not created overnight and that if you are lucky enough to have more than you need, you carefully preserve it. Your expectations for spending and preserving wealth. What do you think the appropriate use of your families' money is?

How long do you expect it to last?

Talk about this with your children and grandchildren so that your expectations are clearly understood.

Wealth is a means to an end, not an end itself. Share with the younger generation that money in and of itself doesn't bring you fulfillment, rather it is simply a tool that helps you achieve your vision of a better future.

Choosing A Sustainable Withdrawal Rate

Do you know what percentage of your assets you can safely spend each year to preserve your wealth indefinitely? For most people, the answer is no. For the past two decades, 4% has been the industry standard for a sustainable withdrawal rate. But recent studies show the 4% rule may not be as conservative as we thought given the current interest yields on bond index mutual funds.

The truth is, your sustainable withdrawal rate depends on many factors, such as your retirement plan horizon, portfolio mix, and risk tolerance. Once created, this rate must be monitored over the course of your lifetime to ensure it remains sustainable.

Have A Solid Wealth Management Plan

Creating sustainable generational wealth is both an art and a science. As we mentioned above, communication with family members is one part of the equation, but the second part involves deploying comprehensive strategies to protect your wealth.

On your plan is where you develop a clear goal that plan the direction of the wealth so it is sustained for future generations. Lacking a proper plan could result in the wealth being lost for future generations to taxes, poor investments and unprepared recipients of the wealth. The plan should be a roadmap providing in-site on how the wealth should be managed and invested for future generations. Bringing in a Financial Planning Professional, one who has the experience dealing with the areas you want to focus on and handling your level of wealth, should be considered here as well. This can help ensure that there will be something for future generations.

Create an outside support system

Considering an impartial trustee is very vital when one is planning for long-term generational wealth. Even with a solid line of communication open and a proper decision-making process in place, there will still be challenges that a family will not be able to handle on their own.

Having an objective third-party point of view could be useful, freeing any discussions from emotions that family members may bring to the table. Having a Trustee can also ensure that your wealth is properly managed and will be distributed properly.

If there are intangible assets involved, a trustee, as a neutral party, can protect the beneficiaries over a longer period of time. They can also mediate over emotional attachments that some family members may have over certain items, items that could eventually lead to litigation amongst the family.

If you've spent decades building your wealth you deserve to have a trusted team in place to protect it long after you're gone. A financial advisor can help bridge the gap between facilitating conversations with loved ones and putting together a strong financial strategy for sustaining wealth.

Most parents find it very difficult to discuss their wealth, and what happens when they're gone, with their children. Whatever the reasons for lack of transparency, the failure to discuss will likely end with such issues like unnecessary taxes, costly estate fees, and possible family strife. Also, by not detailing their intentions, you run the risk of eroding the value of your estate.

The families that do maintain their multi-generational wealth are able to do so by communicating with the next generations in a very straightforward manner. The rules they live by to do this are very simple but not always easy.

Failing to adhere to these results may result as an obstacle to having a successful generational wealth. Below is a list of rules that if not observed obstacles may arise in one's way to generational wealth accumulation.

Share the decision making process.

More often than not, beneficiaries of family wealth are unable to properly manage what they've inherited. Often this is the result of decisions made by the earlier generations regarding the members' involvement with decisions made managing the wealth.

By keeping the next generation out of the decision-making process, can lead to serious dysfunction and a lack of understanding about how wealth is managed. They will lack the skills. Without the necessary core values or understanding of their family's goals, the ability to maintain and grow the wealth is lacking.

It is nearly impossible to pass on family wealth to the generations beyond your grandchildren and there are plenty of statistics that back that up. There are many pitfalls that you can avoid to make sure that your hard work will last well beyond the third generation.

Along with investing wisely and developing a good estate plan, educating the next generations is a crucial element in making your wealth last. Put the values you believe in into practice to sustain your family as well as your fortune.

FINAL THOUGHTS

We have now come to the end of this short e-book on generational wealth. In a nutshell, generational wealth is wealth, or assets, that you pass down through your family from generation to generation, over many years. Family members in successive generations inherit this wealth, benefit from it, invest it, grow it and leave it to the next generation.

The concept of building generational wealth is easy. You simply have to acquire assets or save cash that you don't intend to spend in retirement. Then you pass those assets along to your children when you pass away. This sounds easy in concept but can be difficult to put into practice.

If you can leave behind a notable amount of money or assets, that constitutes generational wealth. Stated simply, people who inherit generational wealth have a significant financial advantage over those who do not. These people likely have the ability to avoid student loans and other types of costly debt.

Setting up a trust and naming a guardian for your minor children will be great for your beneficiaries. This includes naming beneficiaries on any pension funds and retirement annuities, life cover and funeral policies. Structuring your estate so that your assets are preserved for future generations will be of great advantage to your children.

Generational wealth
is vital but it has to be
well- practiced for it to
last.

The end.